Advance Praise for
The House at the Heart of the World

According to the mystics, the Torah was engraved with black fire on white fire. These poetic midrash too. Read them slowly. Spend time in the white spaces. Let the foreignness of the text resonate in silence, and find yourself rewarded.
Jay Michaelson, author of *The Gate of Tears: Sadness and the Spiritual Path*

Each installment of Abe's still small voice is a miniature jewel, poetically illuminating with its delicate facets otherwise hidden elements of each parsha.
Dan Friedman, managing editor, The Forward

Abe Mezrich cuts straight back to the roots of the Midrashic tradition, sermonizing as a poet, rather than idealogue. He can quickly build up sacred spaces in the manner of Eastern haiku-writers, or rhythmically zoom through ideas with tight free verse cadences, familiar to American readers. Best of all, Abe knows how to ask questions and avoid the obvious answers.
Jake Marmer, poet and performer

Direct and accessible, Mezrich's midrashic poems often tease profound meaning out of his chosen Torah texts. These poems remind us that our Creator is forgiving, that the spiritual and physical can inform one another, and that the supernatural can be carried into the everyday.
Yehoshua November, author of *God's Optimism*

The House at the Center of the World

Poetic Midrash on Sacred Space

§

Abe Mezrich

THE HOUSE AT THE CENTER OF THE WORLD
©2016 Abe Mezrich. All rights reserved. No part of this book may be used or reproduced in any manner whatsoever without written permission except in the case of brief quotations embodied in critical articles and reviews.

Published by Ben Yehuda Press
122 Ayers Court #1B
Teaneck, NJ 07666

http://www.BenYehudaPress.com

Ben Yehuda Press books may be purchased for educational, business or sales promotional use. For information, please contact:
Special Markets, Ben Yehuda Press,
122 Ayers Court #1B, Teaneck, NJ 07666
markets@BenYehudaPress.com

ISBN13 978-1-934730-52-2

16 17 18 / 10 9 8 7 6 5 4 3 2 1   20160203

And they shall make a Sanctuary for Me, that I may dwell among them.
-Exodus 25:8

And the Tent of Meeting, the camp of the Levites, shall travel in the midst of the Camp
-Numbers 2:17

In memory of Alan Sonnenfeld

Contents

Introduction — xi

Teruma

How to meet God	2
What are years?	4
What makes us strong	6
Filth	8
What we do with holiness in surprising places	10
Spirituality	11

Titzaveh

How the holiest people are different	14
How we talk with God	16
How we encounter God	18
What we need help with	20
The daily things are sacred	22

Ki Tisah

How pure do you need to be?	25
What if we have no leaders?	26
What is your place if you do not lead?	28
The sin of the calf	30
Torah through mercy	32
You come to God for yourself	34

Vaykhel - Pikudei

How we make things matter	36
How plain life is holy	38
Entering and traveling	40
Speech makes newness possible	42
Restraint brings creation	43
How God commands	44

VaYikra

What is religious experience?	46
How do we approach God with our failings?	48
Why it is good to be incomplete	50
When you matter	52
What is a home?	54
Is there choice in religion?	55
The hidden things are for God	56
What if you are not perfect?	58

Tzav

Constant	62
The service at the altar	63
Changing	64
The role of the holy man	65

Shemini

How we move past tragedy	68
How God talks to us	70

Tazria / Metzora

Intimacies	74
Eyes to see	75
How do we keep piety in check?	76
What is impurity?	78

Acharei Mot / Kedoshim

Holy of Holies	80
Can you discover yourself?	82
What should religion teach us?	84

Why a life of work cannot be secular	86
Where will the past go?	88
What do we do with the past?	90

B'har

Counting	92
How to be free	93
How should we use our senses?	94
When does money become holy?	96

Bamidbar

Are the leaders the most important ones in our community?	99

Naso

What is our community?	102
Why we pray in groups	104
What a community takes	105
God's loners	106

B'haalotcha

Is religion necessarily constant?	111
What is light?	112
Is the past more important than the present?	114
Trumpets	115

More poetry from Ben Yehuda Press	cxvii
About the Author	123

Abe Mezrich

Introduction

1. How do we bring God into the world?

2. When God is in the world, what do we do next?

These are two pressing questions couched within the end of Exodus, and the book of Leviticus, and the beginning of Numbers. That is the section of Torah dealing most closely with the Mishkan, the Tabernacle, God's Tent.

These are not questions we typically associate with this long section of Torah. After all, this section is replete with stark minutiae. The cloth of the Tent, and the cattle and the spices and the bread all sacrificed there. The birds and the vermin and the maladies that render a person impure. The methods of anointing a priest. Among so many particulars, one can forget that we, reading Torah, are on a quest for God.

But these specifics are how we build God's Tent, how we create God's place in this world. And they are symbols full of meaning.

So that, in all these specifics, we answer the questions above.

It is these things: these symbols, that place of God, the questions and the answers and the further questions they open—that this book is about.

Abe Mezrich

Teruma

How to meet God

i
God tells Moses:
Let My altar be of clay
or unhewn stone
untouched by a sword.
*

And God tells Moses,
Let My altar have no stairs:
lest it reveal a man's nakedness
as he ascends.
*

Then God gives Laws of justice:
of treating slaves well
and daughters well,
of being watchful of others' property,
and Laws like this.
*

Soon after, God speaks of the Tent
the people shall make
where God will dwell
with a golden altar,
a copper altar;
and silver,
and tapestry:
a place of beauty.

ii
First, God's altar
will be a simple monument
housed by nothing specific—
it will be of the world.
It will be untouched by a sword:
and so an altar of peace.
It will hide nakedness:
and so a place of dignity.
*

From this altar, we come to God's Laws of Justice.
*

From God's Laws of Justice,
we come to the altars in God's Tent—
ornaments of God's cloistered, gorgeous place.

iii
We come to the God of the world.
He shows us how to care for the world.
Learning to care for the world,
we come to God.

Exodus 20:19 and following

What are years?

i
God tells Noah
to build a great ship
out of *gofer wood*
three hundred cubits long
fifty cubits wide
thirty cubits high
to carry the creatures
through the storm.
*
God tells Moses
to build a Holy Ark
from *shittim* wood
two and a half cubits long
one and a half cubits wide
one and a half cubits high
to carry God's *Testimony*
across the Desert
to the Land.
*
Pharoah asks Jacob
How many are the days of the years of your life?
Jacob
who has had a difficult life
who is old
answers Pharoah:
I have lived one hundred thirty years,
few and bad were the days of the years of my life.

ii
A number is a measure
of material for carrying things:
cubits of wood for voyagers
cubits of wood for holy cargo
years of life for bearing good
or bad.

iii
A number is a question:
With only so much material
so much wood
so many cubits
so many years
—nothing more—
what can we carry
and how much
how will we carry good
and not bad
what is in our power
to justify the measure we have?

Genesis 6:13-16; Exodus 25:10, Genesis 47:8-9

―――――

Title taken from the title of a poem by Marianne Moore

What makes us strong

i
The nation of Amalek comes to attack.
Moses goes up to the hilltop, carrying his staff.
Aaron and Hur go up with him.
Moses lifts his hands up.
And as Moses would lift up his hand,
the people *would* succeed in battle.
But *Moses' hands grew heavy.*
*

So *Aaron and Hur helped* Moses' *hands—*
one holding *from here*
and one *from here,*
and Moses' hands, holding the staff,
stayed steadfast until the sun set.

ii
Aaron's two hands *from here,*
and Hur's two hands *from here,*
and Moses' two hands between them,
and Moses' staff,
all *steadfast:*
it is like the Menorah,
the seven-branched Candelabra in the Temple:
three branches of the Menorah from one side
and three from its second side,
and the seventh pole at the center,
all seven lit *continually,*
for all generations.

Abe Mezrich

iii
It is the source of our light,
our strength:
Many uniting together,
sharing together for the long work.

Exodus 17:8-12; ; 25:32; 27:20-21

―――――

Note: Aaron and Hur holding with two hands is my presumption; the text only says they "helped Moses' hands." Also, the text does not say that Moses held his staff on the hill; only that he went up the hill holding his staff.

Filth

i
God will dwell in the Tent
and we will come to meet Him there
and God gives plans for what the Tent should include,
how it should operate.
*

God says:
You shall make an altar of bronze in the Tent;
this will be the Altar
upon which we we bring our sacrifices;
and you shall make *pans for removing* the *ashes*
that heap up on this altar
from its fires.

ii
Though there are many things in the Tent
—a Table to hold bread;
a Candelabra to shine light;
many things—
this altar is the only part
about which God mentions *ashes,*
or any kind of filth.

iii
We are human,
we make things messy,
our encounters with God become messy,
the place where we bring our sacrifices,
this altar,
naturally
becomes messy also:
it fills with ash.
*
But God does not say:
such a filthy thing as man
has no place in My world.
God says:
come into My dwelling-place, My home,
you, who spill ashes,
you, who are merely human;
you can clear your ashes away once you come,
but build the altar of copper
bring sacrifices to Me upon that altar:
come.

Exodus 27:1-3

What we do with holiness in surprising places

We cover the outside of God's Tent with cloth.
On this cloth,
a whole flap
will run beyond the Tent;
that flap
must be folded back
and on to the Tent again.
*
Much of life is made of this:
finding the holiness
that has gone beyond its borders
and grasping it
and letting it guide you
all the way back to God's Tent.

Exodus 26:1-9

Spirituality

God speaks

from between the two cherubim

sculpted onto the Ark-cover

that rests on the wooden Ark

where the recorded Law

—the list of rules—

is kept.

*

The plain,

the basic

upholds the mystical.

Exodus 25:10-22

Titzaveh

How the holiest people are different

i
The high priest wears bells on his robe
so he will be heard
when he enters before God
and he will be heard
when he leaves.

ii
To merely announce his coming
and to merely announce his going
the high priest could simply ring bells.
He does not need to wear them.
*
More than this:
The high priest still wears bells
even after he has come in before God
and even after he has left—
so the ringing continues even after the moment of his coming
and after the moment of his going,
after the moment of his entry,
of his exit—
the moments that requires announcement.
*
So we must ask
what these bells do.

iii
Not every moment is a revelation.
There are plateaus
and there are valleys
between the heights.
*

Yet the high priest carries the music
of the moment when he comes before God
and the music
of the moment he returns outside,
carrying the closeness to God
back out to the world—
the music of the supreme moments
with him, wherever he walks.
*

He is the man of God.

Exodus 28:31-35
The simple reading of the text may be that the robe *will be heard, and not the high priest. However, ambiguity in the phrasing does allow that it may be referring to the high priest.*

How we talk with God

i
There are words on the High Priest's uniform
that he wears in God's Tent.
His breastplate and his shoulder pads
bear the names of the Tribes.
The gold plate on his forehead reads:
Holy to HaShem.
*

As if to say, in writing:
here is my community;
these people
are *holy to HaShem.*

ii
Within the Ark in the Tent
are the stone Tablets of the Testimony:
the stone Tablets with the writing of God.
And *from above the Ark,*
God speaks:
He tells what He *will command to the Children of Israel.*

iii
So the High Priest brings his words
and God offers words back.
*
So the High Priest comes to God,
not saying:
I am special,
I am different,
I am the holy man;
but saying:
I know my community,
and I know that there is holiness in it—
and God responds.

―――

Section i based on a thought of Rabbi Chanoch Waxman
Exodus 25:22; 28:21,29, 36

How we encounter God

i

Moses sets *chiefs of thousands, hundreds, fifties and tens*
who will *judge the people at all times.*
Until now, Moses has judged the people alone.
Now, he spreads Justice throughout them.
*

Soon after,
God says:
let the people build *a sanctuary for Me,
and I will dwell among them.*
*

When the people participate in justice,
when justice is infused throughout them,
God enters their world.

ii

In the Sanctuary,
the high priest will wear a *Breastplate of Judgment*
which shall bear *the names of the Children of Israel,*
a *permanent remembrance before HaShem.*
*

When the people are part and parcel with Judgment,
when the people are part and parcel with Justice,
God remembers us:
we are interwoven in God's thoughts.

iii
So it is Justice
—our human act
of making the world right—
that makes the world a place that can receive God
and that makes us a people
who can be part of God's world.
*
So that Justice makes the meeting with God possible.
So that Justice must be the precursor
to true spirituality.

Exodus 18:19-26 (quote is a loose translation); 28:15,29

What we need help with

i
When the man and the woman
sin in the Garden
God sends them out.
They are *naked*,
and God sewed them coats.
*
Offering coats, God covers them from shame
and from the dangers ahead.
Because the man and the woman
need God to protect them spiritually
the man and the woman need God
to protect them physically.
They need God so much
there is no difference
between the way they need Him physically
and the way they need Him spiritually:
life without His help
is all one nakedness;
the help He offers
is all one garment.

ii
In God's Temple
the priests wear coats.
In God's Temple
the priests wear pants
to cover their nakedness.
So before they come to God,
they are naked,
they are coatless,
like the woman and the man
vulnerable outside of Eden.

Abe Mezrich

iii
Perhaps this is the awareness
we should always bring,
coming to God:
how we are wholly naked,
how it is through God we are covered.

Genesis chapter 3 (esp. 3:21); Exodus 28: 40-43

The daily things are sacred

i
God says *Let there be light*
and makes light for day
and dark for night
and there is evening
and there is morning
and there are seven days of light
that are the days of Creation.

ii
The priests
shall arrange the Temple Menorah's seven lights
the *permanent flame*
lit *from evening to morning*
a Law that stands forever:
that is how God introduces
the role of the priests,
the ones who make the Mishkan
the dwelling- place of God
into a functioning home.

iii
First you must bathe time in light
first you must make a schedule of light
you must commit to a schedule of light
day in and day out
for weeks into eternity
over and over:
that is how God makes the world,
that is how we build a world of God.

Genesis Chapter 1; Exodus 27:20-21
Based on the philosophy of Rav Aharon Lichtenstein.

Ki Tisah

How pure do you need to be?

There is a water basin in the courtyard to God's Tent.
It stands between the altar and the Tent itself.
The priests purify their hands from it
and purify their feet from it
before they approach the altar
or before they enter the Tent.
*
They enter God's courtyard
hands unwashed
and feet unwashed.
They wash their hands
right there, beside God's altar,
before His Tent.
*
So, perhaps
you need to be clean and pure
to serve before God.

But to walk toward Him,
you only need to be ready
to wash yourself.

Exodus 30:17-21

What if we have no leaders?

i
Moses takes too long
coming down from the mountain
where he is up with God.
*
The people feel helpless
and they say to Aaron:
You
make a new god for us.
*
Aaron molds a calf from gold
and the people dance before it,
saying:
This is the god
who has taken us from Egypt.
*
When God forgives the people at last,
He tells Moses:
Three times a year
the people must come to Me,
to My Temple.

ii
If Moses was the way to God
and Moses is lost,
what can the people do?
The people have no answer to this question.
So they make a new god
to be close to.

iii
But God says:
You have misunderstood.
Everyone can come to Me.
Everyone must come to Me.
My Temple doors
are open wide.

Exodus 32:1-6; 34:23

What is your place if you do not lead?

i
The nation Amalek attacks
but the people fend Amalek off
for as long as Moses' hands are raised.
*

Moses grows tired.
Aaron and Hur support Moses' arms.
Moses' hands held up,
the people drive Amalek back.
*

Later Aaron's sons become priests in God's Tent
which Hur's grandson builds.

ii
Hur is neither Moses nor Aaron,
neither leader nor priest.
Hur supports,
gives strength, provides spaces
so others may lead,
become priests.
Hur makes possible.

iii
Ascending the Mountain,
Moses tells the poeple:
Aaron and Hur are with you;
whoever has a matter
should come to them.
*

But Moses *delays*
coming back down.
The people *do not know*
what has happened to him.
They tell Aaron:
make us a god
to replace Moses.
This *god*
is the Golden Calf.
*

We hear no more of Hur.

iv
When the people tell Aaron:
we want only to be led,
to follow;
we have no place
in making new things possible—
they reject the responsibiltiy
of every plain citizen
they reject the notion of Hur.
And the Golden Calf comes
and they end Hur's story.
*

That is their downfall.

Exodus 17:8-13; 24:12-14; 32:1-6
I may have heard parts of this idea elsewhere.

The sin of the calf

i
Moses is with God, up on the mountain.
The people saw that Moses was…long in coming down
They say: *we do not know what has happened to him.*
They say to Aaron: *make a god for us.*
Aaron melts their jewelry down, he makes the Golden Calf.
*

That is:
Moses is a lone man on a mountaintop with God.
The people wait for him below
and cannot be without him—their one leader—
so they make an idol to fill his place.
*

That is:
The religion of the lone saint
comes to idolatry.

ii
On the mountain, God tells Moses:

> *I have called…Bezalel son of Uri, son of Hur,*
>   *of the tribe of Yehudah;*
> *and I have given also Aholiav son of Akhisamakh,*
>   *of the tribe of Dan*
> *and all the wise-hearted* people

to construct the *Mishkan*, the Tent in which God will
dwell *among* the people.
*
God says: let the people build the Mishkan together,
and I will dwell among all of them.
*
There religion of the people joined together, joined to God
the religion of the Mishkan
—not the religion of the lone saint—
brings God among us.

Exodus 31:1-11; 32:1-6

Torah through mercy

i
God gives the Torah to Moses. But the Children of Israel commit the sin of the Golden Calf. And Moses, in anger, smashes the stone Tablets of the Covenant—the stones of Torah—that God had written.
*
God forgives the Children of Israel. He tells Moses to re-fashion a second set of stone Tablets. He calls Moses back up the mountain.

He gives Moses the Torah again.
*
Moses returns from the Mountain. His face shines.
But Moses does not know that his face shines. The people flee from him. Even Moses' brother flees.
*
Moses calls them back. They return to him. He teaches them Torah.

ii
One imagines that Moses is lonely when the people flee from him. And so his calling them back is more personal than a calling-back-to-holiness alone. He is calling to them because he needs them.

But it is impossible for them to stand before this shining man. And so, until he calls them back, they flee.
*
So there is the guilt of sin. And there is Moses' need of others.

There is an impasse, until Moses calls the people back, overcoming their guilt.

iii
Moses reaches out to the people from his loneliness:
he ignores their sin.
Moses brings them back:
the need for others overcomes sin itself.

That is the essence of Mercy.
*
It is in this way that the Torah is finally given.

Exodus 32:1-6, 19, chap 34-35:1

You come to God for yourself

i
How is the Golden Calf made?
The people take *the gold rings of* their *wives,* their *sons,* their *daughters.*
Aaron takes the rings and casts them into a fire.
And the Golden Calf comes of this.

ii
How is God's Tent made?
God says: let *every person whose heart so moves him*
offer gold and silver and copper and cloth and jewels.
And every man must pay a *half-shekel…for his soul.*
These half-shekels will fund the work of the *Mishkan.*

*

To make the Golden Calf, you hand over your wife's jewelry, your children's jewelry--someone else's jewelry.
To make God's house, you give of your own *heart,*
of your own *soul.*

iii
You can come to the Divine yourself.
Or you can expect that others will come to the Divine for you.
*
Which of these options you choose
is the difference between the path to idol-worship
and the path toward the house of God.

Exodus 32:1-6; 25:2; 30:11-16

Vaykhel - Pikudei

How we make things matter

i
Here is what we know
about how they made the Golden Calf:
they snatched their wive's gold
and Aaron melted it
and a calf came.

ii
Now here is what we know
about how they made God's Tent:
We know the cloth
and the wood
and the metals
and the dimensions
and the craftmanship
and who was in charge
and who volunteered
and the Torah tells much of this
over and over.

iii
An idol is useless
so what it is made of
is rendered useless,
and the building of it
is a useless act.
None of it
bears mention.
*

If you put the materials of the earth
and the materials you own
and the materials you create
and your skills of making
to God's work,
all of it
is worth talking about
because all of it
becomes holy.

Exodus 25-40; 32:1-6

There are details to the Golden Calf that I have left out, but I think my point is valid nonetheless.

How plain life is holy

i
God *came down* to the Mountain *in fire*.
and the Mountain *trembled*
and the people *trembled*
and the people *stood from afar.*

ii
Before Moses instructs the people
as to how to build the Tent
—where God *will dwell among them*—
Moses says:
Do not light a fire in your dwelling-places on Shabbat.
That is:
on Shabbat, there is no terrifying fire,
no Mountain,
no Heavens
from which holiness comes down.
There is only your *dwelling-place,*
your home,
God's day.
*

That is the thought
which the people must contemplate
as they begin making a dwelling-place for God.

iii
From above,
God shines so bright it is terrifying.
But if we bring God down to us,
amongst us,
God becomes not terrifying
but constant and enveloping and strong:
like a home.

Exodus 19:18, 25:8, 35:3

How a leader creates a people

i
God tells Moses to command the people
to donate materials
and craft the parts
that will make up God's Tent,
God's home.
*
When the people finish this work—
when they have given their materials
when the expert craftsmen have crafted
when the masterful women have woven cloth—
God says to Moses:
you, now,
take these parts
that the people have made
and assemble them into My Tent,
My home.

ii
A leader is one
who finds the amazing things
that each of the people offer
that each of the people can make
with the gifts they own
with the talents they have within them.
He knows how
when these parts come together
when these people come together
they can become something incredibly holy:
they can become a home for God.

Exodus 35:4 and following; 40:1 and following

Entering and traveling

i
At Sinai, God descends in a *thick cloud* and summons Moses.
Moses ascends the Mountain and is alone with God.
*

When the Mishkan
—the dwelling- place of God—
is completed, Moses tries to enter it.
He is *not able to enter...: the Cloud* of God's Glory is there.
*

Trying to enter the Mishkan—where the cloud is,
where God is,
Moses tries to repeat what he had done before,
at Sinai,
standing intimately with God,
within the Cloud.
Now he cannot.

ii
Now, here is how the people travel the Desert:
When the cloud was taken up from upon the Mishkan,
the Children of Israel went onward in all their journeys.

Through the Mishkan,
the Cloud is no longer a sign for being alone with God.
It has become a signal
for the whole nation's journey with God.
No wonder now Moses is *not able to enter* alone on account
of the Cloud.

iii
There is a time to be alone with God.
There is a time to journey with God, out with others in the wide world.
This is so, even if the transition feels as if God Himself has shut you out.

Exodus 19:16, 40:34-38; translation mostly from Koren

Speech makes newness possible

i
The people offer materials
with which to build the dwelling-place of God.
But when the people bring their gifts *each morning*
and there is too much material
too much silk, scarlet, purple, wood, gold, silver, brass,
the craftsmen say: *The people bring… more than enough
material for the work.*
So it is *proclaimed throughout the camp* that no more gifts
should come.
And the gifts stop. The work begins.
*

The Hebrew phrase *proclaimed throughout the camp* literally
means: *they passed a voice through the camp.*

ii
Here is a community of the steadfast.
It brings gifts *each morning*.
In the face of such steadfastness, how can there be newness?
That is a trouble for the craftsmen, who look to build
something new: a new house to God.

iii
They passed a voice through the camp.
Now words pass *through* the people.
The mass of the community becomes vibrant and liquid
with speech.
In the fluiditiy of speech,
something new can come.
Now building can begin.

Exodus 36:1-7

Restraint brings creation

i
Moses commands the Children of Israel to build the *Mishkan*, God's dwelling place. He begins with the command to keep the Sabbath day. This places Sabbath as central to the creation of God's House. This places cessation of work as central to the creation of God's House.
*
Another forced cessation: after the Children of Israel volunteer up more material for the Mishkan than is necessary, Moses tells them to stop bringing.

ii
The first level of creation is to pour your full life into the created thing.
And God breathed into Man *the breath of life.*
But what you create will not become itself
until you stand away.
This is creation through self-restraint.

iii
It is like the spirituality of Law: that is a spirituality of self-restraint.
Through that self-restraint, you create a space for God to enter: you build a *Mishkan*.
*
This is also what God accomplished in His *tzimtzum* at the Creation of the World. He made Himself small and the Universe, that did not have the strength to carry Him, could exist in His presence.

Genesis 2:7; Exodus 35:1-3,36:1-7

How God commands

i
God tells Moses of the home the people shall make for
Him.
Moses tells the people
and the people construct the pieces
and Moses assembles the pieces
into a home.
And God comes down to dwell there.

ii
From God to Moses to the people to Moses to God.
*
Sometimes God's command
is also a dialogue.

Exodus Chapters 35 - 40

VaYikra

What is religious experience?

i
God tells Abraham to sacrifice his son
but suddenly reveals a ram
to offer instead.

ii
One would think that,
to honor this story,
we would sacrifice ram upon ram in God's Temple.
But we offer rams rarely:
only if a man misuses Temple property
or sins without realizing
or swears falsely
that he does not have another man's things;
and on special holidays.
Mostly we offer sheep,
lambs, goats, doves, flour.

iii
Had Abraham sacrificed his son,
he would have parted ways completely
with his life.
Perhaps, then, the ram is a symbol
of stepping out of life:
as when you encounter holy property too closely,
or sin without knowing,
or assume another man's things,
his person;
or on special holy times.

iv
If we rarely offer rams in the Temple,
our meeting place with God
perhaps it is to tell us how
if we stray from life
on the way to God,
it can be wrong
or it can be special
but either way
it should be rare.

v
That is:
we are meant to encounter God primarily
not from another life—
but from the life we have,
the life God gave us.

Genesis 22:1-19; Leviticus 5:14-26; Numbers 28:1-30:1

How do we approach God with our failings?

i
Isaac will bless his older son,
Esau,
whom he loves most.
He will not bless his other son,
Jacob.
*
Rebecca,
the sons' mother,
dresses Jacob in goat- skins
to make him hairy to the touch
(as Esau is)—
so Isaac,
old,
blind,
will feel Jacob
and think he is Esau
and bless him.
*
So that the goat represents a way
to become someone other than yourself:
to become someone more loved than yourself.

ii
Amongst the first things God lets us know
about Temple sacrifices
is this:
If you bring Me an offering *of your flocks,*
you may bring it
of the sheep or of the goats.
*
Inviting the sacrifice of a goat,
God invites us to disguise ourselves,
perhaps,
as one He loves more.

iii
Approaching God,
one of our first questions is:
Who am I to approach Him?
God answers:
Even if you do not deserve
this closeness,
disguise yourself as one who is very righteous
who is very holy
who is very deserving of God.
Pretend you are such a person.
So that no matter who you are,
you may come to Me.

Genesis 27:1-40; Leviticus 1:10

Why it is good to be incomplete

i. *Pieces*

God's Tent
is described thus:
many boards
many curtains
many cloth pieces
many vessels
brought together.
*
When you offer God an animal
you offer blood
you offer fat
you offer kidneys
you offer the tail.
When you offer God grain
you separate out
a portion of the grain
to go on the altar,
another portion of the grain
for the priest to eat.
When you offer God bread,
you break the bread.

ii. *Fragments*

A thing that is whole
cannot connect
to something else
to someone else.
A thing that is whole
cannot connect
to God.
It is whole,
it leaves no room.
*

Fragments have room.
Fragments can connect.

iii. *Israel*

A person of Israel
is part of a family
is part of a tribe
is part of the nation of God.
He is only a fragment.
Because he is a fragment
he is special.

Exodus 25:1 and onward; Leviticus 1:1 and onward
―――

For simplicity's sake and to draw out the theme from the text, I have dealt with the sacrifices as if they were uniform across all animals / bread offerings. (Also note that the text suggests that not all bread offerings are broken.)

When you matter

i
God speaks
of the man who brings a sacrifice
in God's holy Tent:
how he lays hands on the animal
and slaughters it before God.
And God speaks
of how after the priests sprinkle the animal blood
and prepare the animal parts
they must set the fire on the altar
and lay wood on the fire
and lay the animal on the fire.

ii
First comes the man
who comes to God.
Then comes the priest
with God's fire.
*

This is the opposite
of the Creation of the world,
that begins with God's Light
and culminates in Man.
Here, it is a person
who triggers God's flame.

iii
Here is the amazing dialogue:
Our world begins with God's Light;
when we come to God
we let God's Light begin.

Leviticus 1:1-9
I have read this according to the simple reading of the passage, but the Halakha is clear that the flame is constantly on the altar. See Leviticus 6:5-7 and Maimonides Temidin Umusafin Chapter 2.

What is a home?

i
Cain gives a *gift*, a *minchah*, to God.
Abel, too, brings his *minchah*.
God accepts Abel's *gift*
and rejects Cain's.
Cain kills Abel.
*
In God's Tent, too
— in the Tent
all Israel built
from material they offered together,
from the work they shared—
there, too, you can bring a *minchah*,
a *gift*,
before God.

ii
When every man is for himself
in a world of winner-take-all
in the world of Cain and Abel
there cannot be enough plenty
enough good
enough love to go around.
Even a *gift* comes to violence.

iii
A home is an inversion of this.
Together we take a small place
and make it a wide world.
*
Sometimes, that place
is large enough to house God.

Genesis 4:1-8; Leviticus 2:1-4

Is there choice in religion?

i
God says:
In the Mishkan,
the holy place
where the people meet God,
when any of you presents an offering to HaShem,
you may bring it
of the herd
or of the flock.
*
If you present it *of the flock*, then you shall ready it *on the side of the altar, to the north.*

ii
Often, place is relational:
- before Pi-HaKhirot, between Migdol and the sea,
before Ba'al Tzefon.
But in the Mishkan, place is not relational.
Place is absolute.
There is a *north*.
God's home is a place of absolutes.

iii
But in the Mishkan, too,
God offers choice:
one gives *of the herd or of the flock.*
*
In fixedness,
choice comes.

Leviticus 1:2; Exodus 14:2

The hidden things are for God

i
Cain kills his brother, Abel, and hides him in the ground.
God asks Cain: *Where is Abel, your brother?*
Cain answers: *Am I my brother's keeper?*
*

To say:
I am not responsible
for what is wrong in the world
that is hidden from me,
that I have hidden.

ii
The people build the Mishkan,
God's dwelling-place
in the people's midst.
God says:
when you hide things unlawfully
- When you keep your neighbor's lost object but deny that you have it
- When you could testify in court but claim you know nothing
then you must bring an atonement-sacrifice
in that Tent.
*
With God's dwelling-place in your midst,
you cannot hide from things.

iii
The hidden things are for HaShem, a later verse says.
If we share a part of God's house, His realm,
then we share the hidden realm with God.
*

And Cain's answer is not possible any more.

Genesis 4:1-9; Leviticus 5:20-26 *(but note how order is switched)*; Deuteronomy 29:28

What if you are not perfect?

i
God tells us of the sacrifices
we must bring in God's Tent,
God's home.
*

First He speaks of the sacrifices we bring
as gifts of the heart.
Then He speaks of the sacrifices we bring
as acts of penance.
*

We begin addressed as the pious ones.
We end addressed as sinners.

ii
Perhaps this ordering is so
because the closer you get to God
the more your sins matter:
the more perfect you become
the more imperfect you are revealed to be.

iii
But perhaps, also,
it is that a home is something you come to in love
and a home is the place you come back to
after you wander away.
Once you say:
This is my home,
you are always welcome—
perfect,
imperfect,
it does not matter.
*
And we make God's home
into our home:
so that perfect,
imperfect,
we are always welcome,
we are always at home,
whatever we are.

Leviticus Chapters 1-5

Tzav

Constant

The altar is the place
where man approaches God.
A fire burns *continually* upon it.
We give offerings twice daily upon it.
*

So that our encounter with God
comes not in a grand encounter
but in seeking that holy rhythm—
day in, day out.

Based on the thought of Rav Aharon Lichtenstein
Leviticus 6:1-6

The service at the altar

i
The priest must *raise the ashes* up from off of the Altar,
and place the ashes down *beside the Altar*.
He wears the *linen garments* of his priesthood.
*

Then he must *remove his linen garments*
and *put on other garments*
and *carry the ashes* away, outside the camp, to a pure place.

ii
The world is holy at the Altar and *beside* it.
The priest lives in that world.
*

But even so, at times the priest *removes his linen garments*
and *puts on other garments*.
He must seek the *pure place* that is far from the Altar.
This is also part of the service of the Altar.

Leviticus 6:3-4
Inspired by Rav Yair Kahn's reading of Parshat Korach

Changing

i
The priest who brings an offering upon the Altar,
in the Temple, *shall put on his* priestly *linen garment.*
He shall remove his garments when he leaves the Temple.
He shall put other garments on.

ii
The priest puts his garments on, and he takes them off again.
He serves in the Temple, and he goes away.
He comes and he goes.

iii
Such a man must know that his life is in flux.
He must know that his life can change.
*
Perhaps it is precisely such a man who is called to serve in God's Temple, at God's Altar.

Leviticus 6:3-4

The role of the holy man

i
The Torah speaks of the Laws of sacrifices
first from the vantage-point of the people
who bring sacrifice
and then from the vantage-point of the priests.
*
The Torah opens the discussion
of the vantage-point of the priests
with the elevation-offering:
The priests set a fire continually before God
and the elevation-offering is to be burnt in that fire
and after the offering has been burnt
the priests are to take the ashes away.

ii
The Torah does not mention here
the elaborate preparations the priest are to do
for the sacrifice itself.
The focus is, simply,
on the priests setting the fire
and clearing the ashes,
tending the altar
for the people's service.

iii
That is how the Torah
introduces the vantage-point of the priests.
*
Perhaps to say:
the role of the holy man
is not to be the focus of the religion
but simply to set the stage for others
who want to approach God.

Leviticus 6:1-6

Shemini

How we move past tragedy

i
Aaron's two sons die in God's Tent,
bringing *a strange fire*
they were not meant to.
*

There in the Tent,
that world of men,
we hear no word of their mother.

ii
Suddenly God tells Aaron
and his remaining sons
to tend to women after childbirth
and to leprous women;
to teach Laws of menstruation.
*

Then *after the death of Aaron's sons*
God introduces Yom Kippur—
the day sins are forgiven
and Aaron
and every high priest afterward
enters God's chamber.
*

The Talmud says:
only a high priest who is married
may conduct that service.
So in a way,
a woman, too,
enters God's chamber.

iii
God creates Man *alone*.
Woman is the Other
whom Man must recognize
to make him complete:
bone of my bones,
flesh of my flesh.
*

So that here, perhaps is the message:
Tragedy is an incompleteness
like being alone,
like manhood.
And a spiritual life of aloneness,
of sheer manhood,
is tragic.
*

The only way past tragedy,
past the incompleteness,
is through embracing the other
through the woman
who can make us complete, at last, again—
ourselves
with each other
with God.

Genesis 2:23; Leviticus 10:1-2, Chapter 12-16 Mishnah Yoma 1:1

How God talks to us

i
God speaks of the animals we may eat
and the animals we may not:
we may eat
cloven-footed beasts that chew their cud;
insects with jumping legs
like crickets, grasshoppers, locusts;
we may not eat
rabbits, pigs, eagles, owls, mice.
*

God says we may eat
any creature of the water
with fins and scales,
but no other water- creatures.
*

God mentions beasts, birds, vermin by name.
He mentions nothing of the water by name.
For creatures of the water,
God mentions only qualities.

ii
Perhaps this is because
God speaks to a desert people.
In the desert,
the people know beasts,
birds,
vermin.
But the sea is far away.
Water and the fish and the animals in it
are far away.
So perhaps these people
have many names for beasts,
birds,
vermin—
but few names
for the creatures of the sea.
*
So God does not mention
the creatures of the water
by name;
God merely describes.

iii
To say:
God does not speak to us
in spiritual codes
in lofty constructs;
God speaks to us
in the language we speak
in the lives we live,
as the people
we actually are.

Leviticus Chapter 11

Tazria / Metzora

Intimacies

i
The text speaks of Laws of food.
And then the text speaks of Laws of childbirth.
Then the text speaks of Laws of skin, and clothes, and houses.
Then the text speaks of Laws of touching between people.
*
Then the text speaks of Laws that are kept
between a woman and a man.

ii
Then we see the Laws of how the High Priest, on Yom Kippur, must enter the Holy of Holies—the room that is God's chamber.

iii
We learn to live in our small world.
We learn to be with each other in that world.
*
This education brings us, finally,
to the intimate space of God.

Leviticus chapters 11 - 16

Eyes to see

i

Of all the people who know us, it is we who know ourselves the least *(Kundera)*.

Our eyes are not mirrors.
*

We live in a community. But we cannot know, truly,
how we make others feel.
We live before God. We cannot see ourselves through God's eyes.

ii

Tzara'at is a group of skin disorders. One who thinks he
has *tzara'at* must come to the priest. The priest will say if the
skin-sickness is *tzara'at*.
If the skin-sickness is *tzara'at*, then the stricken one is impure.
But only after the priest has declared
that the skin-sickness is *tzara'at*
does the stricken one become impure.
Even if a man knows that he has *tzara'at*, he is not impure
until the priest says that he is.

iii

The priest is of the community.
The priest is a man near to God.
The priest holds the vantage- point that we do not.
*

The priest is the one who declares us impure.
The priest is the one who tells us if we are pure.
He is the one who tells us what we are, what we have become.
*

To know ourselves, we must learn his vantage-point.

Leviticus chapter 13; Maimonides Laws of Leprosy 9:2

How do we keep piety in check?

i
When a man is cured of the skin-sickness
the priest guides him back to purity:
The priest *shall command* that *two birds* are taken,
and he *shall command that one bird be slaughtered,*
and he *shall send the living bird loose into the open field.*
Then the skin-sick man returns to purity.

ii
On Yom Kippur,
the day we are forgiven,
the High Priest takes two goats
and puts his hands in a box
and *casts lots on each goat*—
one *for HaShem,*
to be sacrificed;
one to be sent away
by another priest
to a barren land.
And we are forgiven.

iii
The priest purifying the man
*command*s that a bird be slaughtered
and sends the second bird away himself.
The High Priest's goats
are chosen by chance—
which is to say: by God—
and another man sends the second goat away.

iv
How do we bring purity?
We *command* the world:
we shape, force the world into something religious.
*
But also we say:
the world is not ours to shape,
it is not ours,
the world is God's.

Leviticus 14:1-8, 16:1-22

―――――

I am indebted to Rav Ezra Bick for the underlying metzorah / Yom Kippur parallel.

What is impurity?

i
If a person will have skin-sickness,
then the priest will isolate him
and check back later again;
and if the person's *rash has spread on the skin,*
then this person is *impure.*

ii
The *rash* spreads in isolation.
It gains strength in a life distanced from all others.
*
Here is impurity.

Leviticus 13:1-8

Acharei Mot / Kedoshim

Holy of Holies

God tells how the High Priest may enter the Holy of Holies,
the innermost holy chamber of God's Temple:
the place that is so holy, it is a wonder that a man should ever
be allowed to enter into it.

God says: the High Priest must enter the Holy of Holies
each year, on Yom Kippur.
*

Yom Kippur is the day on which you ask how far
you can progress into the world of God.

You enter into the place which is the answer to that question.

Leviticus chapter 16

Coats

i
The Creation was simply an expression of God's want.
Let there be…and there was.
But when God created the man, the man ate the Fruit.
And God sent the man, naked, into the world.
*
Then God gave the man and his wife *coats; and God dressed them.*
*
Sinning, the man worked against God's Creation.
God sent him away.
Dressing the man, God said: even so, I will care for you.

ii
Rosh HaShanah is the anniversary of God's creating Man.
It is also the day on which God judges us.
It is like the time when God asked, *Have you eaten of the Fruit?*
*
After Rosh Hashanah, Yom Kippur will come.
God will let us atone for our sins.
God will say: even so, I will care for you.

iii
Creation and Rosh HaShanah and Yom Kippur
  tell the same story:
God will clothe us in our nakedness, despite everything.

Genesis chapter 1 -3, esp. 3:21

Can you discover yourself?

i
God tells us: *you shall be holy*:
- Revere *your father and mother.*
- Do not mix wool thread and linen thread in a single garment.
- When you plant a tree, let it grow for four years before you take its fruit.
Honor other people, other things, for what is unique in them.
*

Honoring others, you cannot say: I am the center of the world.
Honoring others, you say: These others aside from me matter.

ii
God says: *you shall love* the immigrant *like yourself,*
for you were immigrants in the land of Egypt
(coming to Egypt in Joseph's time,
fleeing hunger).
Do not say: I am very different from others.
Even with those who come from far away,
say: They are like me.

iii
So others become the focus of the world—and not you.
And you do not cut yourself off as different from all others;
you *love* others,
you know you are one of them.
*

You do not discover yourself.
You discover the world,
you discover that you are a part of the wider world.
This is what you must discover
if you are to *be holy.*

Leviticus 19:1-24

Emor

What should religion teach us?

i
God lists the year's holidays.
He begins with Passover,
the holiday of the first month
of the Bible's year
(not like today,
our calendar beginning
at Rosh HaShanah).
He ends with Sukkot
and Shemini Atzeret:
joint holidays
in the seventh month,
the month when the holidays end.

ii
God speaks of the Exodus in this list.
But not in the context of Passover,
when you would expect.
He mentions the Exodus
with regard to Sukkot.
He says:
Dwell in *sukkot*—huts;
remember how I *made the Children of Israel
dwell in huts
as I took them out
from the Land of Egypt.*
*

Not: *How I struck Egypt with Plagues.*
Not: *How I split the Sea.*
Simply:
How I made them *dwell.*

iii
At the culmination of all holidays,
we do not come
to a revolutionary understanding
of the single moment
when God changed the world.
We come to know
the day after:
how the miracle must suffuse
the ways we are,
how we act,
where we wander.
How from that miracle
we are to make homes to live in,
lives to lead.
Sukkot in which we *dwell*.

Leviticus chapter 23

Why a life of work cannot be secular

i
From the first month
to the seventh month
is our time of work:
it is the time,
in Israel,
from planting to harvest.
*
From the seventh month
to the first month,
it is the rainy season.
*
And the *first month* and the *seventh month*
are the only two months
in which there are specific dates for holidays.
Passover in the first month,
Rosh HaShanah, Yom Kippur, and Sukkot in the seventh.
(No actual date is given for Shavuot.)

ii
So a festival time
and five months of work
and a festival time;
a festival time
and five months of God's rain
and a festival time.
*
It is like two sets of festivals,
like two Passovers—
which starts with a day of *holy gathering*,
and ends on the seventh day
with a *holy gathering*,
and has five work days in between.

Abe Mezrich

iii
Our part of the year
is a festival of working the land
and God's part of the year
is a festival of watering the land.
*

From these two festivals together,
the earth blooms.

Leviticus 23:5-25
Obviously, I only refer here to holidays mandated within the Torah—
and not to Purim or the Rabbinic holidays.

Where will the past go?

i
Two men of Israel fight in the Desert.
One is of Egyptian descent. The other is of pure Israelite lineage.
The man of Egyptian descent blasphemes God.
God commands that he be put to death.
Then God also says: *You shall have one system of Law for the foreigner and the citizen alike.*

ii
The People has carried its Egyptian past,
a past among heathens,
all the way with it into God's Desert.
So they bear great contradiction:
Israelite, Egyptian,
heathen, holy.
These opposing parts struggle
with one another.
*

And God says:
the Egyptian blasphemer,
that relic of your past,
must be taken away.

But God also says:
there is but one Law
for citizen and foreigner;
citizen and foreigner
are both equals in the Law,
are both part of the community:
the otherness
is still a part of you
that should stay.

iii
Rav Soloveitchik said:
sometimes our past is so sinful,
we must reject it.
At other times,
we can transfrom our past that we have left
into a part of our holy present.
*
In that interplay—
taking the past away,
bringing it close—
we form a religious life.

Leviticus 24:10-23
See Soloveitchik on Repentance *by Pinchas H. Peli*

What do we do with the past?

i
On Sukkot you live in huts:
so your generations may know that God *made you dwell in huts, when* He *took you from Egypt.*
*

Sukkot comes at the harvest-time, *when you have gathered in the fruit of the Land.*
And on Sukkot you take four plants of the Land of Israel:
a citron, a palm-branch, a willow, a myrtle
—*and you rejoice before your God.*
*

On Sukkot you remember how God took you from Egypt—
into the Desert, toward the Land.
And you celebrate the Land, the harvest, God has brought you to.
You live in the past and the present, at once.

ii
Here is the lesson:
Each moment—the past, the present—offers its unique relationship with God.
We do not let go of these relationships.
We gather them together.
We do not stand reinvented before God.
We stand enriched by the past with God.

iii
In the Torah's calendar, Sukkot comes at the close of the holidays (Passover begins the holidays).
A year's holidays are ending.
At the end of all this time, we are ready for Sukkot's lesson.

Leviticus chapter 23:39-44; "and you rejoice before your God" is a paraphrase.

B'har

Counting

i
To count toward a whole is to note how the many small pieces add up, how they converge to construct a world.
*

We are commanded to count out seven cycles of seven years, culminating in the Jubilee year.
*

Seven is the number of days in which God made the universe.

And so seven is the number that contains all things.
And so our counting to the Jubilee year is a kind of counting toward infinity.

ii
In the Jubilee year, slaves return, free, to their clans.
In the Jubilee year, real estate that has been bought and sold is reclaimed by the clans as ancestral land.
All the places and people we have seen as chattel up until now are resettled, at long last, in their places within the families that make up the nation.

iii
To be made to count is to be made to see that infinity is made of many tiny numbers,
and the people and the places we saw as mere numbers are what make up the mosaic that is our people.

Leviticus Chapter 25

How to be free

i

Every fiftieth year, on Yom Kippur, the shofar is sounded in the Land. Real estate goes back to its first owners and slaves go free.

For God has said: *the Land may not be sold off permanently, for the Land is Mine.*
And God has said: Your brethren may not be sold into a true *sale of slavery, for they are My slaves.*
*
All things are God's. To acknowledge this is to make all pretense of ownership fall away.
Things are freed. People are freed.

ii

Repentance comes after you declare that your rebellion against God was a fiction of the mind. That your rebellion against God was a rebellion against Truth.

For all of life is God's: and so your life outside of God was a fiction.

In declaring this, you consecrate to God the life that was always His. In the same way that sounding the shofar on the fiftieth year gives back to God the things that He already owns.

iii

Such a declaration is the beginning of atonement.
We make such a declaration each year on Yom Kippur, that is the *Day of Atonement.*
We set ourselves free.

Leviticus 25:8-24,42 (but note the order of ideas in verse 42)

How should we use our senses?

i
I see the world from my own vantage-point.
But I hear your voice
from any direction;
sound calls me to you.
*

Consider:
Eve finds the Fruit
a pleasure to the eyes;
but she and Adam *hear*
the voice of God in the Garden,
and they know they have wronged Him.
Eyes are a gateway to your pleasure;
sound startles you
from yourself
toward another.

ii
We count out forty-nine years.
On the fiftieth
we blow the *shofar*,
the trumpet.
Debts are forgiven,
land reverts to ancestral families,
land goes fallow;
slaves go free.
To say:
your borrower
your land
your slave
have their own existence
apart from yours.
*

We come to this understanding
through the trumpet:
through listening.

iii
Of the slave who shall go free
in the fiftieth year,
God says:
he is owed freedom,
you shall not see him worked brutally
before your eyes.
To say:
train your eyes
to find brutality
to root it out.
*
For forty-nine years
you ready yourself to hear the shofar:
to listen,
to hear around you.
Learning to listen,
you learn to use your *eyes*.
Learning to listen,
you learn to see.

Genesis 3:6,8; Leviticus 25:8-28,53

When does money become holy?

i
God says: *When you come to the land,* every seventh year
you must renounce ownership of the land
and share that year's *produce* with *your servant* of every kind
and with your animals that labor with you
and with the animals of nature.
*

And God says: *If you follow My Laws…*
I will grant your rains in their season;
and *the Land shall give forth its yield.*
*

Then God tells the Laws
of how a person may donate money
—*value*—
to God's Temple.

ii
We think of our wealth
as our own.
But if you share your wealth
with the community around you,
and if you know your wealth comes
only through God's *rain*—
then your wealth can truly hold *value,*
then your money can be made holy to God.

Leviticus 25:2,6; 26:3-4; 27:3

Bamidbar

Are the leaders the most important ones in our community?

i
There is a passage naming the clans of the tribe of Levi, and the *prince* of each clan, and the role each clan will play in tending to the holy things.
*
Nestled in this passage:
> And the prince of the princes of Levi is Elazar,
> the son of Aaron the priest; he shall be *in charge of
> those attending to the duties of the sanctuary.*

Elazar shall oversee the doings in God's holy place.

ii
Elazar is the *prince of the princes*.
He oversees the workings of the sanctuary of God.
Yet there are other princes, clans, tasks mentioned before him.
And there are other princes, clans, tasks mentioned after him.
He is one among many.

iii
Perhaps this is to say:
> A leader is just one of many roles.
> There are many princes, clans, tasks.
> There are many roles to play.

Everyone has his role to play.
Everyone has his work to do for God.

Numbers 3:32

Naso

What is our community?

i
God tells Moses
to gather the tribal leaders
to take a count
of the people.
The word that God uses
for this counting is
si'u:
lift up.
*

In the Desert
these people who have been counted
encamp around the Priests,
many of whom *will lift up*
the pieces of God's tent
to carry the Tent
through the Desert.
*

When the Priests bless the people,
their closing phrase is:
May HaShem lift up
His face to you
and give you peace.

ii
We *lift* each other
from the blur of the masses
to become counted people.
*

We, a community
of counted people
lift up God's Tent
from the level of the ground
to a point above the earth.

Abe Mezrich

*
We who raise God's tent
call upon God
to *lift* His face up,
to *lift* Himself up
making our lives
lives of peace:
lives of treating others
as more than a blur of masses
but as people who are counted.

iii
In respect for each other
we ready our lives
to bear the holiness
that readies us
to bear God—
Who guides us
to respect each other.
*
This cycle
makes up our community.

Numbers 1:1-19, 4:24-27, 6:24-27
I have heard this use of "being counted" in reference to this census elsewhere—perhaps from Rabbi Yosie Levine.

Why we pray in groups

i
The Torah speaks twice of the completion of the building
of God's Tent.
*
In the first telling
(at the close of the Book of Exodus)
God comes to the Tent
and Moses cannot enter—
because who can come before God?
But then God calls to Moses
and speaks to him.
*
In the second telling (in the Book of Numbers)
the Princes of the Tribes of Israel
volunteer gifts,
donations for the Tent from each tribe.
And following the Princes' gift-giving
Moses walks into the Tent,
and God speaks to Moses.

ii
Alone, you wait for God's grace.
But the entire people can march up to God's Tent.
Following the people,
you can come to the place of God,
to the place where God speaks to you.

Exodus 40:35, Numbers Chapter 7

What a community takes

i
God commands a nationwide census.
And He arranges how each tribe will encamp
as the nation travels across the Desert, and into the Land.

Then He commands the Laws of one who has committed
wrong against his fellow's property.
> The *wrongdoer shall make restitution in full.*
> And he shall also pay *a fifth* of the extent of
> the harm, as a fine.

ii
What is one man's sin against another,
and the *restitution* of it,
doing just here
—just after the discussion of organizing a nation, and
mobilizing a nation?
*

Perhaps here is the answer:
> Because people will wrong one another.
> So you cannot build a community without showing
> people how to right their wrongs.

*
You cannot build a community without showing it how to
heal itself.

*Numbers 5:5-10. The text is slightly ambiguous so I have
read it to refer to any financial wrongdoing, but there is strong
reason to say it refers specifically to wrongfully taking holy
property.*

God's loners

i
It is just before Moses finishes
building God's Tent,
God's home among the people.
*

God tells Moses:
let the ones who are sick
with the sickness of impurity
leave the camp.
(When they are pure again
they will return
and bring sacrifices
in God's Tent.)
*

God tells Moses:
a jealous husband
can come with his wife
to God's Tent
to face her.
*

God tells Moses:
a person may become a *nazir*,
a holy monastic—
not a priest
not a prophet,
but one set apart.
And the *nazir* must comes to God's Tent
when his time as a *nazir* ends.

ii
Before Moses finishes building
God's Tent,
God mentions these lonely ones
—the sick and alone
—the jealous, alone from their spouses
—the seeker, alone with God—
who all come to the Tent.
*

You might think:
this Tent,
this nation's home for God,
has no place in it
for people who do not fit in the nation.
Before the Tent is finished,
God says:
even these outsiders
have a place in My Home,
even they
have a home with Me.

Numbers 5:1-6:21

B'haalotcha

Is religion necessarily constant?

i
The cloud of God rests upon the Tent of God.
The people encamp around the Tent, around the cloud.
When the cloud lifts up, the people follow it.
They follow the cloud until it rests down to the ground again,
and the people reunite with it again.

ii
The cloud rests and rises up,
rests and rises up,
throughout the forty years in the Desert.
And the people follow the cloud all the way to the Land.

iii
The people do not come to the Land by encamping steadily around the cloud.
They do not come to the Land by resting steadily with God.
They come to the Land in the continual process
of being apart from God's cloud
and reuniting with it,
of parting and reuniting,
over and over for forty years.
In this cycle, they arrive.
*
They come to the Land in the continual process
of being apart from God
and reuniting with Him,
of parting from Him and reuniting,
over and over for forty years.
In this cycle, they arrive.

Numbers 9:15-23

What is light?

i
In the Beginning, God says: *Let there be Light.*
> *And there was Light.*
> And God *separated* the Light from the Darkness.
> He *separated* the *waters above* from *the waters below.*
> He *gathered* the *waters to one place,* so *dry land* would *appear.*

*

God creates
through the Light
that illuminates difference:
light from darkness,
above from below,
dry land from water.

ii
God commands that the High Priest light the Menorah
—the candelabra—
in the Temple.
Then God tells the people:
you must separate the Levites
from among the Children of Israel.
The Levites will serve in the Temple
in place of the firstborn,
whom God chose
when he struck the firstborn in Egypt
and not the firsborn of Israel.
*

Light of the Menorah
and then separation:
firstborn from other children,
Israel from Egypt,
Levites from the rest of Israel.
Light,
separation.
Like Creation all over again.

iii
God illuminates distinctions in the universe,
creating a universe.
God says to us: you, too, must illuminate distinctions
—uniqueness—
amongst peoples,
creating humanity.

Genesis 1:1 – 2:3, Numbers 8:1-19

Is the past more important than the present?

i
At Israel's freedom from Egypt,
God says:
conduct the ceremony of the Passover lamb
now and this time every year
to recall how God freed you from Egypt.
*
The next year
at the same time
God mobilizes the people
from Mount Sinai
and into the Desert
and toward the Land.
God says:
conduct the ceremony of the Passover lamb.
But He makes no mention of Egypt at all.
*
So the Passover lamb is tied to the past,
and the Passover lamb is tied to the new journey.

ii
History is what has happened;
but what is unfolding now is also our history.
*
Both call for ritual,
both call for tying history back to God.

Numbers 9:1-5

Trumpets

i
The Cloud of God rests upon the Tent.
When the Cloud lifts up
the people continue the journey,
following the Cloud through the Desert.
*
You would think that this would be the only signal
the people need to wander on.
But Moses is to make two Trumpets
that the priests will blow
to announce the time for *the journeying of the camps.*

ii
To move following God's Cloud
is to follow a vision of God.
This is a great good.
*
But perhaps it is better
to makes God's vision
into your own trumpeting,
your own music.
If you could do this
then to follow God's vision
you must learn to follow yourself.
Perhaps this way of following things is best.

Numbers 9:15-10:10

*More poetry from
Ben Yehuda Press*

"Barenblat's God is a personal God - one who lets her cry on His shoulder, and who rocks her like a colicky baby. These poems bridge the gap between the ineffable and the human. Her writing is clear and pure and the poems are exquisitely executed. This collection will bring comfort to those with a religion of their own, as well as those seeking a relationship with some kind of higher power."
— Satya Robyn, author of *The Most Beautiful Thing* and *Thaw*

Geshem: Prayer for Rain

Millennia ago, the earth was washed in water
connections sparked unimaginable across the water

the life we know begins cradled in water
each human being emerges in a flood of water

from ancient times we've prayed to God for water
not too much, not too little, just enough water

this year the landscape I first knew lacked water
grasslands parched, thirsting for drops of water

this year the hills where I live ran with water
seeping through roofs, swelling doors shut with water

to mark holy times we immerse ourselves in water
washing our old hurts away in water

in the city of gold rooftop tanks collect water
those who have and those who lack fight over water

in the beginning, presence hovered over water
mysterious and unknowable like deep water

the bodies we inhabit are made of water
our veins and tissues stay functional through water

we couldn't stand and offer praise without water
source of all, be kind to us: send water.

"Sue Swartz does magnificent acrobatics with the Torah in *We Who Desire*. She takes the English that's become staid and boring, and adds something that's new and strange and exciting. These are poems that leave a taste in your mouth, and you walk away from them thinking, what did I just read? Oh, yeah. It's the Bible.
—Matthue Roth, author, *Yom Kippur A Go-Go, Never Mind the Goldbergs, My First Kafka,*

SLEEP ON A BED OF STONES

The deadliest season since climbing began, storms
claiming twelve with sudden vengeance. Frozen bodies
are left on the slopes, human cairns teasing the next
expedition and the next.

Sherpa or American, nationality means nothing
at twenty-seven, eight, nine thousand feet where limbs
twist in on themselves from air tenuous as love.

Everything is foreseen, though free will is given—

You quote me Akiva when I insist no one
has any business on that slickness of mountain,
skating the unbounded ice fields—

And gift me a box, small and unadorned by ribbon
or bow, the avalanche of angles a delight
to your mathematician's eye. White on white borders
bleed one into the other, perfect cube marked only
by the space it is not.

I turn the box in my hand,
feel for the intersection where one edge begins
and another ends.

Perhaps it isn't madness that propels us to approach
the clouds, wings spread wide, but desire—

To transform hard corners into soft & slippery planes,
just as air whooshed into a cube will spill its secrets
onto the jagged horizon, white against dazzling color,
white against white against white.

We Who Desire

About the Author

Abe Mezrich is a graduate of Yale University—where he studied creative writing with the novelist Robert Stone—and of Yeshivat Har Etzion. Mezrich's work has appeared in *The Jewish Daily Forward*, *Urim v'Tumim*, and *Zeek*. A native of New Jersey, he now lives in Los Angeles with his wife and two sons.

Read more of his work at TorahParsha.com.

www.ingramcontent.com/pod-product-compliance
Lightning Source LLC
LaVergne TN
LVHW041338080426
835512LV00006B/516